DARK PSYCHOLOGY

AND

MANIPULATION

The Ultimate Guide to Learn about the Manipulative Behavior and to Defend Yourself from It

By

Jake Bishops

Table of Contents

Introduction 9
What Do Manipulators Want? 10
Chapter 1. Knowing Dark Psychology 11
How Dark Psychology Is Used Today? 11
Dark Psychology Tactics That Are Used Regularly 12
Love Flooding 12
Lying 13
Love Denial 13
Withdrawal 13
Restricting Choices 13
Semantic Manipulation 13
Reverse Psychology 14
Who Will Deliberately Use Dark Tactics? 14
Narcissists 14
Sociopaths 14
Politicians 15
Salespeople 15
Leaders 15
Selfish People 15
Wide, Practical and Theoretical Observations 16

The Code of Hammurabi 17

Chapter 2: Psychology and Dark NLP 21

Personality Does Not Go Away 24

What You Need to Know 26

Play on Hope and Fear 27

Insult Someone Subtly 28

Chapter 3. Characteristics of Manipulative People 30

How Manipulators Select Their Victims 31

Signs of a Manipulative Partner 33

How to Know You Are Being Targeted 35

How to Deal with a Manipulator 36

Chapter 4: What is Emotional Manipulation? 38

Specific Types of Emotional Manipulation 39

Lying *40*

Lying by Omission *40*

Denial *40*

Rationalization *40*

Minimization *40*

Diversion *41*

Evasion *41*

Covert Intimidation *41*

Guilt-tripping 41

Shaming 41

Blaming the Victim 42

Playing the Victim 42

Playing the Servant 42

Seduction 42

Projection 43

Feigning Innocence 43

Feigning Confusion 43

Peer Pressure 43

Signs That You're Being Manipulated 44

Specific Examples of Emotional Manipulation 46

Chapter 5: Victims **49**

Traits of a Victim 49

Empathetic 50

Caregiver 50

Codependent 51

Grew Up in Dysfunction 52

Low Self-Esteem 52

Signs of Abuse or Manipulation 53

Self-Sacrificing or Martyrdom 53

Self-Sabotage *54*

Fiercely Protective of Abuser *54*

Mental Health Issues *55*

Being Distrustful *55*

Fearful Behavior *55*

Paranoia *56*

Chapter 6: Stop the Manipulators 57

Chapter 7: Dark Criminals among Us 65

Criminal Mind vs. Cybercriminal Mind 67

The Role of Psychology in the Legal System 67

The Roles of a Criminal Psychologist 69

Clinical *69*

Experimental *69*

Advisory *70*

Actuarial *70*

Profiling *70*

Applied Criminal Psychology 72

The Dark Triad 73

Chapter 8: How the Mind Works When It Is Manipulated 76

Using Isolation to Get What You Want 76

Criticism 78

Alienating the Target to Get What They Want 80

Using Social Proof as a Form of Peer Pressure 82

Conclusion **83**

© Copyright 2021 by Jake Bishops - All rights reserved.

This book is provided with the sole purpose of providing relevant information on a specific topic for which every reasonable effort has been made to ensure that it is both accurate and reasonable. Nevertheless, by purchasing this book, you consent to the fact that the author, as well as the publisher, are in no way experts on the topics contained herein, regardless of any claims as such that may be made within. As such, any suggestions or recommendations that are made within are done so purely for entertainment value. It is recommended that you always consult a professional prior to undertaking any of the advice or techniques discussed within.

This is a legally binding declaration that is considered both valid and fair by both the Committee of Publishers Association and the American Bar Association and should be considered as legally binding within the United States.

The reproduction, transmission, and duplication of any of the content found herein, including any specific or extended information, will be done as an illegal act regardless of the end form the information ultimately takes. This includes copied versions of the work, physical, digital, and audio unless express consent of the Publisher is provided beforehand. Any additional rights reserved.

Furthermore, the information that can be found within the pages described forthwith shall be considered both accurate and truthful when it comes to the recounting of facts. As such, any use, correct or incorrect, of the provided information will render the publisher free of responsibility as to the actions taken outside of their direct purview. Regardless, there are zero scenarios where the original author or the publisher can be deemed liable in any fashion for any damages or hardships that may result from any of the information discussed herein.

Additionally, the information in the following pages is intended only for informational purposes and should thus be thought of as universal. As befitting its nature, it is presented without assurance regarding its prolonged validity or interim quality. Trademarks that are mentioned are done without written consent and can in no way be considered an endorsement from the trademark holder.

Introduction

'Dark psychology' is a term some people make use of to refer to the darkest or most disturbing traits a person may have, such as so-called Machiavellianism.

This term of dark psychology has also encompassed undesirable personality traits, such as the manipulation and control exercised over another person, among others, which, besides, are dangerous if the other person does not know how to fight since he or she could become a victim.

Mental manipulation is associated with taking control of an individual's or a group's behavior through techniques of persuasion or psychological pressure. The manipulator attempts to eliminate the person's critical judgment by distorting his or her reflective ability.

Through various techniques, the manipulator succeeds in influencing the actions, thinking, and emotions of the subject. The manipulation can be developed in any type of environment and relationship. Manipulative relationships exist inside families (father-son, mother-son, husband-wife, etc.), but also in many broad contexts (such as the manipulation exercised by a political leader on his followers).

A crude situation of manipulation occurs when a mother tells her son that, if he behaves well, Santa Claus will bring him presents at

Christmas. This is a minor manipulation, which does not cause harm, but includes the presentation of a fictitious reality to a subject (the child) who believes in the words of the other (the mother).

A riskier manipulation takes place when a social leader presents a biased view of reality to induce a certain behavior in the village, by blaming immigrants for economic problems, for example.

What Do Manipulators Want?

They just want to:

- Shut down your willpower: They want to raise doubts in your mind and keep you under their protection.
- Tear down your self-esteem: They're not helpful; they're only trying to bring out your flaws.
- Passive-aggressive revenge: They want you to be punished by ignoring you. When you are in need, they push you away.

Chapter 1. Knowing Dark Psychology

Psychology is going to underpin everything in our lives from advertising to finance, crime to religion, and even from hate to love. Someone who can understand these psychological principles is someone who holds onto the key to human influence.

This is not an easy task which is why most people don't possess it. Learning all the different principles of psychology is not necessary. Start with the lessons on these pages, and you'll have a solid foundation. You have to be able to read people, understand what makes them tick, and understand why they may react in ways that may not be normally expected. And even then, you may need to spend time taking classes and reading through countless books to gain a complete understanding. It depends on how far you want to go with this.

So, if only a few people understand psychology and how the human mind works, why is it so important to know what this is? It is because those who do know what it is and how to use it can choose to use that power and that knowledge against you.

How Dark Psychology Is Used Today?
While some people are going to use these dark psychology tactics to harm their victim, there are times when you may use these tactics without the intent of negatively manipulating another

person. Some of these tactics were either unintentionally or intentionally added to our toolbox from a variety of means that could include:

When you were a child, you would see how adults, especially those close to you, behaved.

When you were a teenager, the mind and your ability to understand the behaviors around you were expanded truly.

You were able to watch others use the tactics and then succeed.

Using the tactics may have been unintentional in the beginning, but when you found that it worked to get you what you wanted, you would start to use those tactics intentionally.

Some people, such as a politician, a public speaker, or a salesperson, would be trained to use these types of tactics to get what they want.

Dark Psychology Tactics That Are Used Regularly
Love Flooding
This would include any buttering up, praising, or complimenting people to get them to comply with the request that you want. If you want someone to help you move some items into your home, you may use love flooding to make them feel good, which could make it more likely that they will help you. A dark manipulator could

also use it to make the other person feel attached to them and then get them to do things that they may not normally do.

Lying

This would include telling the victim an untrue version of the situation. It can also include a partial truth or exaggerations to get what you wanted to be done.

Love Denial

This one can be hard on the victim because it can make them feel lost and abandoned by the manipulator. This one includes withholding affection and love until you can get what you want out of the victim.

Withdrawal

This would be when the victim is given the silent treatment or is avoided until they meet the needs of the other person.

Restricting Choices

The manipulator may give their victim access to some choices, but they do this to distract them from the choices that they don't want the victim to make.

Semantic Manipulation

This is a technique where the manipulator is going to use some commonly known words, ones that have accepted meanings by both parties, in a conversation. But then they will tell the victim later on, that they had meant something completely different when they used that word. The new meaning is often going to change up the entire definition and could make it so that the conversation goes the way the manipulator wanted, even though the victim was tricked.

Reverse Psychology
This is when you tell someone to do something in one manner, knowing that they will do the opposite. But the opposite action is what the manipulator wanted to happen in the first place.

Who Will Deliberately Use Dark Tactics?
Many different people may choose to use these dark tactics against you. They can be found in many different aspects of your life, which is why it is so important to learn how to stay away from them. Some of the people who can use some of these dark psychology tactics deliberately include:

Narcissists
These individuals are going to have a bloated sense of their self-worth, and they will need to make others believe that they are superior as well. To meet their desires of being worshipped and adored by everyone they meet, they will use persuasion and dark psychology.

Sociopaths
Those who are sociopaths are charming, intelligent, and persuasive. But they only act this way to get what they want. They lack any emotions. This means that they have no issue with using

the tactics of dark psychology to get what they want, including taking it as far as creating superficial relationships.

Politicians

With the help of dark psychology, a politician could convince someone to cast votes for them simply by convincing these people that their point of view is the right one.

Salespeople

Not all salespeople are going to use dark tactics against you. But it is possible that some, especially those who are really into getting their sales numbers and being the best, will not think twice about using dark persuasion to manipulate people.

Leaders

Throughout history, there have been plenty of leaders who will use the techniques of dark psychology to get their team members, subordinates, and citizens to do what they want.

Selfish People

This could be any person that you come across who will make sure that their own needs are put before anyone else's. They aren't concerned about others, and they will let others forego their benefits so that they can benefit. If the situation benefits them, it is fine if it benefits someone else. But if someone is going to be the loser, it will be the other person and not them.

This list is important because it is going to serve two purposes. First, it is going to help you be more aware of the people who may try to manipulate you to do things that you don't want to do, and it can be there to help out with self-realization.

Wide, Practical and Theoretical Observations

Murder, rape, incest, abuse, all words that can send chills up your spine. As a culture, we have saturated ourselves with negative ideals for entertainment purposes. We sit and watch horror movies, crime shows, and reality shows diving into the minds of the deviant. The darkness within these becomes an obsession for some, and though they don't reenact or find the actions preferable, there is a connection that few want to recognize outwardly. While the majority of human beings have a buffer in their mind, knowing fact from fiction and right from wrong, some lack it.

Imagination is one thing. Combing through the worst fears of people to find what scenario can be the scariest and most grabbing is something that fiction writers and creators do. Often though, when watching these dark psyches at work on the screen in front of you, the human mind finds certain recognition of why the predator or villain did what they did. Some movies and books even prey on the idea of the worst human condition. Depraved and distraught, the father who witnessed his family's murders climbs out of his ominous depression to wreak havoc on those that committed the acts to begin with. There is a satisfaction for people in the revenge of heinous acts. But then, doesn't that apply the same dark psyche to the perpetrator, regardless of the reasoning behind it?

Dark Psychology has no pointed targets and cares little for the reasoning behind the actions. It is the actual act of manipulation, deceit, and harm that carries the weight within the dark psyche. The idea of revenge has been around a very long time, and at some significant points in history was considered a requirement of honor if the wrong was done to you. Very clear examples of the "eye for an eye" concept are still in existence today. The death penalty is one such example, though the root of it is wide and doesn't currently encourage private actions of one person to another. The federal organization as a whole is in charge of carrying out the punishment. But long before that, laws were erected in civilizations that based themselves on the idea of revenge.

The Code of Hammurabi

The Code of Hammurabi dates back to Babylonian times. Around 1760 B.C., the king of Babylon set forth a stone pillar inscribed with the laws of his kingdom. They are considered the oldest discovered set of laws in our history as human beings. What is so significant about the Code of Hammurabi? It is the fact that it is set in the pure idea of revenge. King Hammurabi believed wholeheartedly in the idea of an eye for an eye and set forth over thirty laws of Babylon based on that specific theory.

Through time, this code has shown its influence through almost all judicial and legal systems. Even the American justice system is predicated on the idea of an eye for an eye. A punishment system where retribution for a crime is equal in severity to the crime committed. What was not expected or understood was the fact that this revenge system is actually internally governed by a specific part of our brains called the dorsal striatum. This sector controls the idea of revenge within our minds. For victims of crime, the dorsal striatum is more active. So ultimately, with a society of an eye for an eye, we are taking the actions of a dark psyche and melding a new one from their actions.

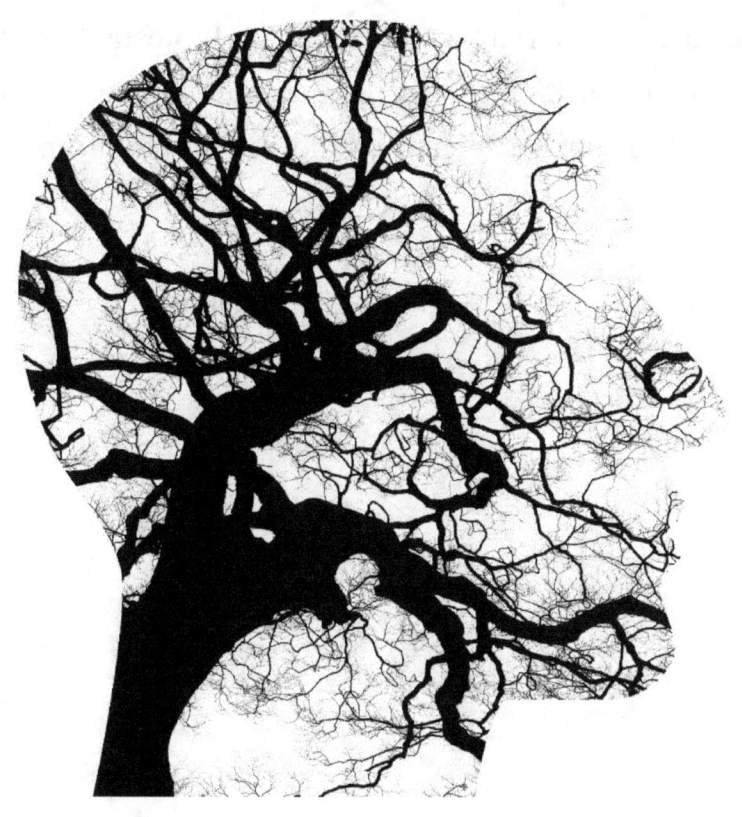

One very prominent case of revenge on a large scale would be the St. Bartholomew's Day Massacre. This massacre occurred during the Protestant Reformation in the sixteenth century. During this time, a new sect of Christianity had been created, and the Catholic Church stood to lose control and power over people, land, and money. In August 1572, the French Protestants flooded Paris for the marriage of a Catholic woman to a Protestant aristocrat. When the wedding was over, King Charles IX ordered that the aristocrat be killed for his crimes to the church. To make it as easy as possible, he also ordered the murder of the Protestants within the town and then outward into the French countryside. That case of revenge cost society between thousand and four thousand lives.

Chapter 2: Psychology and Dark NLP

One of the many fundamental lessons of the Enneagram is that psychological incorporation and spiritual recognition are not different steps. Away from our spirituality, recognize that psychology might not relieve us or direct us to the inmost realities about ourselves, and with no psychology, spirituality can head to grandiosity, misconception, and an effort to escape from real life.

The Enneagram is not dry psychology, neither fuzzy mysticism nor an instrument for improvement that employs the clearness and perceptiveness of psychology as a point of entry into a deep and common spirituality. Therefore, in an actual sense, the Enneagram is "the link between psychology and spirituality."

The foremost of this hallowed psychology is that our fundamental type discloses the psychological mechanisms by which we overlook our real nature—our divine essence—how we leave ourselves. Our personalities draw on the capabilities of our ingrained temperament to build resistance and compensations for where we've been harmed in early childhood. To endure no matter what difficulties, we all experienced during those times, we unknowingly figured out a limited collection of techniques, self-images, and habits that enabled us to deal with and thrive within our early environment. Every person consequently has become an "expert" at a certain type of coping which, when used overly, also gets to become the core of the dysfunctional aspect of our personality. As the barriers and methods of our personality get more organized, they cause us a loss of nearness to our direct experience of ourselves, our essence.

The personality ends up becoming the origin of our identity instead of contact with our being. Our experience of ourselves depends more and more on internal images, thoughts, as well as practiced behaviors instead of on the natural expression of our real nature. This loss of nearness to our essence leads to deep stress and anxiety, using the model of one of the nine passions. Once established, these passions, which happen to be commonly unconscious as well as hidden to us, start to drive the personality. Knowing our personality type, as well as its dynamics, accordingly offers a specifically potent strategy to the unconscious, to your pains and compensations, and eventually, to our recovery and improvement.

The Enneagram lets us see where our personality most "trips us up." It stresses simultaneously what's feasible for us, and how self-defeating and needless a lot of our old responses and conduct are. This is precisely why, when we finally identify with the personality, we're settling on becoming far less than who we are. It's like we had been offered a mansion to reside in, with luxurious furniture and beautifully kept grounds, but have restricted our-self within a smaller dark closet within the basement. Nearly all of us have even ignored that the other parts of the mansion are obtainable, or that we're actually its possessor. As spiritual instructors from the centuries have remarked, we've fallen asleep to ourselves and also to our personal lives. Much of the time, we walk around obsessed with ideas, worries, uncertainties, as well as mental images. Hardly ever are we present to ourselves and also to our immediate experience.

While we continue to fix ourselves, conversely, we start to see that our focus has been exploited or "magnetized" by the preoccupations and attributes of our personality and that we are in fact sleepwalking through most of life. This particular view of things is as opposed to common sense and frequently feels insulting to how we see ourselves—as self-determining, mindful, and in command. Simultaneously, our personality is not "bad." Our personality is an integral part of our development and is particularly essential for the refinement of our fundamental nature.

The issue is that we end up being stuck in personality and don't understand how to continue to the next stage. This isn't the outcome of any inherent flaw in us; instead, it's arrested development, which happens simply because almost no one in our developmental years was conscious that a lot was possible. Our parents as well as instructors perhaps have had some glimmers of their real nature; but like us, they usually did not identify them, much less live as expressions of them.

Personality Does Not Go Away

The objective of the Enneagram is merely not to allow us to remove our personality. In case we could manage to, it won't be very useful. This is comforting to those individuals who worry that if we get rid of our personality, we'll lose our identity or perhaps become less competent or efficient. In fact, exactly the opposite is true. Once we make contact with our essence, we do not lose our personality. It becomes more transparent and flexible, something that helps us live rather than something that takes over our lives. We are most existing and alert—attributes of essence—while the manifestations of our personality often times cause us to disregard issues, make a few mistakes, and make dilemmas of all sorts.

NLP, neuro-linguistic programming, is a fascinating approach to persuasion and communication that works. Invented by Bandler and Grinder in the 1970s, NLP has since developed into a multi-billion-dollar industry that many people turn to for guidance. The methods taught by NLP help people learn how to banish bad memories, improve their cognition and mood, and learn to cope with mental issues, and even seduce or communicate better with other people.

The great thing about dark NLP is that it applies to all areas of life. You can use it for seduction, persuasion, deception, or even making yourself more confident and powerful. You can use it in romance, friendship, career, or family. You are invincible in all areas of your life when you start to use dark NLP.

NLP is built on the premise that you create the world around you. The way that the world appears to you is created through information filtered through your five senses, your speech patterns, and thought patterns taught to you when you were little. Some of your behavior is very unhelpful, but you can use NLP techniques to change this behavior and develop healthier habits.

You can use visualization, meditation, and even hypnosis on yourself to correct your maladaptive behavior habits. You can basically get into your own head and change your basic thought habits. NLP allows you to restructure your thinking and erase bad memories using your senses, language, and self-talk.

But based on this logic, you can also use NLP to enter the minds of others and restructure their thinking. And this is exactly what dark NLP entails. Dark NLP takes helpful NLP practices and flips them on other people. Dark NLP can be used for good or evil. Either way, it gives you significant control over others by allowing you to rewire their brains and affect their thinking.

Using dark NLP, you break people's behavior down into simple parts. Then you affect change by showing people how to behave differently. You use subtle influence to make people think about their actions and approach situations differently. Dark NLP essentially provides a tunnel directly into someone's mind. You can access their mind with simple techniques like the sensory stimulus, gestures, and phrasing words in certain ways.

Encouraging people to envision things and to think in new ways also enables you to change their thinking effectively.

And the best part about NLP? It is performed through simply nuances in speech or sensory stimulus. Therefore, it is undetectable. You can gain control over someone and he will never guess that you are the reason he is changing.

What You Need to Know

You need to know a few things about a person before you can make him change. You need to learn what he likes about himself, what he hates about himself, what he wants, what he fears, and what he has doubts about. These are essentially the elements of his identity, but they are also weak points. When you target them, you can change them? You can hurt someone through his doubts, fears, and dislikes, or disable him by removing all the things that he likes about himself and hopes for. You can also persuade or seduce him by playing on what he wants or scare him into action by provoking his fears. Do you understand now why these five things are so important to using dark NLP?

Take some time to get to know your victim before you employ dark NLP. Pay attention to what he does and says. The things that he talks about provide dead giveaways into what he feels and who he is. He will avoid what he fears and get nervous about what he doubts. He will get excited and brag about his hopes and his sources of pride. You will find plenty of clues into his identity if you just open your ears and listen carefully.

You can also coax someone into sharing themselves with you by talking about yourself. Share your own hopes, fears, doubts, and self likes and dislikes. When you open up, you establish a trusting bond. You also make him want to reciprocate. Listen to how he responds to you and pay attention to what he chooses to share with you.

You can find out someone's insecurities and pride by complimenting him. He will preen himself if you mention something that he likes about him. He will get rather shy and even hesitant to thank you when you compliment something that he is insecure about. This information is crucial to owning your victim.

Play on Hope and Fear
Play on someone's hopes and fears using your word choices. When you want to influence someone to act a certain way, you want to show him how it might be related to his hopes and how it will benefit him. On the other hand, remind him of his fears about an action that you want him to avoid.

You can also frame his perspective based on his hopes and fears. Use positive, upbeat language that relates to what he hopes for, or wants. For instance, if you want someone to date your sister, you want to paint a visual of your sister that includes all the things that this person hopes for in a partner. "She's kind, she loves to give love and compliments." Then you can flip this and hint that his worst fears will come true if he dates someone else that you don't want him to see. "She tends to emasculate men."

Play with someone's hopes and fears by offering them what they want and then confronting them with what they fear. This emotional roller coaster is confusing and also makes people insecure. They don't know which way is up when they are forced to experience so many different emotions. Fear and hope are two very powerful emotions, so using them simultaneously will have an impact on people emotionally.

Insult Someone Subtly

An obvious insult will make someone hate you. But subtle insults allow you to shatter someone's self-esteem while appearing innocent. Find out what someone hates about himself. Then mention that every now and then in a subtle way. Don't ever make a direct or obvious insult. Disguise your insults as compliments, even.

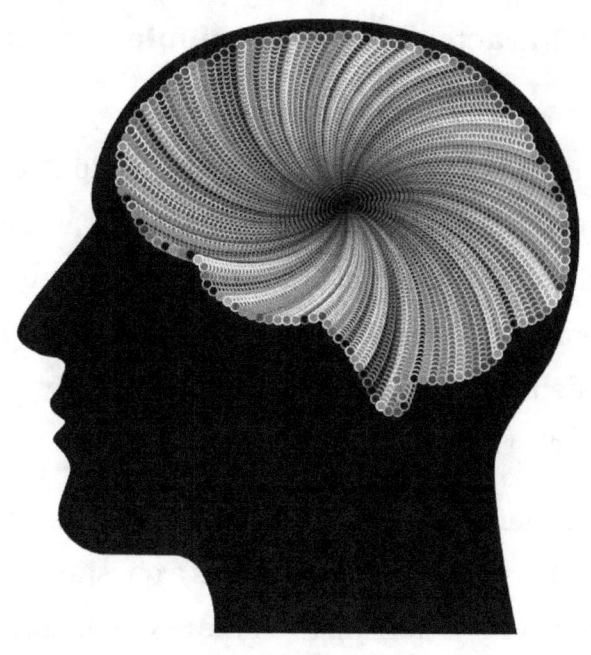

Chapter 3. Characteristics of Manipulative People

The main traits that are associated with manipulators and how they can control people around them. Moreover, we have focused on how personality traits that lean toward manipulation tend to manifest themselves in an individual. That's why we have gone into great depth in analyzing how and why the average manipulator acts the way they do.

On the whole, there is a debate whether being a manipulator is a question of in-born traits or whether it is a question of upbringing. In other words, we're referring to a nature vs. nurture debate. The fact is that there is no conclusive evidence linking specific genetic predisposition to acting in one manner or another. While traits such as psychopathy can be linked to actual physiological conditions in which the individual's brain may differ significantly, the fact of the matter is it is almost entirely an issue associated with upbringing.

For most folks, manipulative traits, such as the dark triad, are fomented in early childhood and adolescence. When kids and teens are subjected to certain types of experiences, they generally develop coping mechanisms that grow into the personality traits that we associate with manipulation. For instance, narcissism is generally linked to abandonment issues, which typically translate into a need for control. Of course, this isn't an iron law. But it does show that there is a clear correlation between the experiences that a child and teenager may go through, and how that translates into certain behavioral patterns down the road.

Therefore, it's important to analyze all aspects of a person's life to determine where one set of traits may emerge. It can be rather foolish to dismiss the effects of the environment on a person's behavior. In fact, many folks make a rash judgment in saying that manipulators, or even psychopaths, are just "born that way." The fact of the matter is that while there may be a physiological component (mental illness is a hereditary issue), most of the time, manipulative traits are the result of a certain set of experiences that a person goes through from an early age.

How Manipulators Select Their Victims
One of the most important things to consider in this discussion is how manipulators select their victims. A victim, by definition, is the recipient of the manipulator's actions. Therefore, the victim suffers negative consequences from the behavioral patterns exhibited by the manipulator.

On the whole, victim selection is generally random. This means that manipulators will simply sniff around, looking for someone they can take advantage of. When there is a greater amount of premeditation in the selection of a victim, then we might be dealing with a psychopath. As such, these individuals might make more careful study as to the type of person they seek to attack.

Nevertheless, most manipulators will simply seek out those who are closest to them. This is why family tends to be the first target on a manipulator's radar.

Generally speaking, manipulators look for weak individuals whom they feel won't be able to put up a fight. This means that for one reason or another, the victim is powerless to stop them. When you think of physical violence, this is one of the main criteria that goes into the selection of a victim.

On a deeper, more emotional level, manipulators will seek out people who stand to lose quite a bit more than the manipulator.

Think about that for a moment.

Let's go back to the example pertaining to the workers who must deal with a manipulative boss. In the end, the workers need the job far more than the boss does. If anything, the boss manipulates the employees more for personal pleasure than a logical business reason. Consequently, the workers are faced with a dilemma: they either put up with the manipulation or find another job.

The ultimate objective of the manipulator is to subdue their victims to the point where they will offer resistance to the manipulator's tactics. This means that the victim eventually becomes complicit in the manipulator's behavior. Sure, there are instances where the victim is unable to extricate themselves from the abusive situation they are in. In such cases, the victim can only hope to endure the situation until a time comes when they are able to get out finally.

Highly skilled manipulators will take the time to scout for potential victims. This occurs when a manipulator is able to identify the choice traits they are looking to find in their victims. As such, they will scout their surroundings and places they perceive will have the highest number of vulnerable individuals. That is why it's always a good idea to be skeptical of someone you don't really know in a place that you often go to. You never know who you might be dealing with.

Signs of a Manipulative Partner
One of the objectives on the mind of a manipulator might be to find a partner they can manipulate. This may occur either as a conscious behavior or an instinctive one. In the event of instinctive behavior, you can assume that the manipulator is not acting out of malice, but rather out of their own sheer desire. When you consider a conscious choice on the part of the manipulator, then you might actually be dealing with an evil individual who has a hidden agenda. So, it is important to recognize the warning signs before it is too late.

On the whole, manipulators can be easily spotted in romantic relationships by the subtle hints and lapses they show. For example, they appear to be sweet and attentive, but suddenly change and appear to be disconnected. You can tell this by seeing the way they pay attention to your conversation. Also, they might be very polite and caring but suddenly react abruptly when something that they don't like happens.

These are very subtle signs that you are dealing with someone who might not be entirely forthcoming. But the red flags get worse when you're dealing with someone jealous and possessive. This can begin with incessant text messages and calls. It's a progressive matter; they start off by increasing the number of calls and texts until you find that they are controlling everything you do. Eventually, they expect a tally and report of all the things you do.

Besides, a manipulative partner will strive to find out things that are negative, embarrassing, or even traumatic about your past. Then they will use that every time they can. For instance, a manipulator may use their partner's weight as a means of shaming. They will use this to coax their partner to comply; after all, "no one will love you as much as I do." These types of statements are a clear indication that there is a manipulation attempt.

These red flags are important to keep in mind as they can quickly degenerate into an abusive relationship. Highly skilled manipulators will make the transition so subtle that the victim won't even notice the relationship is degrading to that level. In the end, all the victim can feel is the effects of the abuse.

How to Know You Are Being Targeted

It can be hard to know if you are being targeted by a manipulator. Perhaps the easiest way to go about this is to confront the manipulator. If you happen to run into someone who is overly friendly, then this ought to be a red flag for you. Also, if you happen to be surrounded by people who only remember you every time they need something from you, then you know you're definitely being targeted.

Unless you know a person well, it's always a good rule of thumb to keep an eye out on everyone. While this may seem like paranoid behavior, the fact of the matter is if you are able to be alert, the chances of being nabbed by manipulators are rather slim.

Here are some practical tips:

- Be wary of overly friendly strangers.
- Watch for offers and deals that are "too good to be true."
- Keep an eye out for sudden mood swings.
- Watch out for contradicting behavior and words.
- Pay attention to the moment in which people approach you.
- Avoid responding to unsolicited advice.

These situations are all indicative of a manipulator trying to "test" you. If they find that you are responsive, then they may feel compelled to continue their advances until you give in to what they want. In the end, it's usually best to just get away from these people. You may never have to engage them openly; all you may have to do is just move away from them.

How to Deal with a Manipulator

If you happen to find yourself dealing with a manipulator, here are three very important steps that you can take to help you better deal with this type of individual.

Try your best to get away from the situation. While there are circumstances in which getting away from a manipulator may be virtually impossible, it is the most recommended course of action to get away from them as far as possible. This will take away their opportunities to manipulate you. Moreover, if you can completely extricate yourself from a situation (such as finding a new job), then the entire better.

Find out what they are using to manipulate you and then take it away from them. If you can identify what they are using against you, then you will be able to take that weapon away from them. In fact, you may even be able to use it against them. That will be a clear indicator of the manipulator that they can't have their way with you any longer.

Know your rights. If you happen to be in an abusive relationship or situation, you have the right to seek help. This can be any form of help that may be available to you, but you must act on it. If you know you are being affected by a manipulative and even abusive person, but fail to say anything about it, you may never get the help you need. So, it's important to speak up.

Avoid the blame game. Do not think for a second that this situation is your fault. Also, there is no need to blame the manipulator, even though they are responsible for their actions. When you play the blame game, you are hurting yourself by making it seem that you are directly, or indirectly, responsible for what's happened. So, even if you are the victim, it's not your fault that this has happened to you. By the same token, the manipulator is not at fault for being a manipulator. However, they are responsible for their actions.

Know when to quit. If you choose to confront the manipulator, you need to know when you may need to get away from them. There is only so much energy you can spend on a person like this. Oftentimes, dealing with a manipulator becomes a war of attrition. So, your determination to win that war may leave you more spent, both physically and emotionally, than what you stand to gain.

Chapter 4: What is Emotional Manipulation?

You've likely experienced individuals who are emotionally manipulative and controlling.

They utilize these practices to get their direction or prevent you from saying or doing anything they don't care for.

Emotional manipulation can be unpretentious and misleading, leaving you befuddled and wobbly.

Or then again, it tends to be clear and requesting where fears, disgracing, and remorseful fits leave you shocked and immobilized.

In any case, emotional manipulation isn't worthy, and the more you enable it to proceed, the more force and certainty the manipulator gains in this uneven relationship.

Inevitably, any leftover of a sound association is pulverized, as the establishment of trust, closeness, regard, and security disintegrates under the sled of manipulation.

Specific Types of Emotional Manipulation

Within these major categories of emotional manipulation techniques, psychologists have also identified a wide range of more subtle variations that we all likely encounter daily.

These techniques include:

Lying

Dark Triad personalities, particularly psychopaths, are highly skilled at lying and cheating, so often we may not detect their intent until it is too late. Beware of those who have demonstrated a pattern of dishonesty.

Lying by Omission

Lying by omission is a little more subtle. The predator may not say anything that is untrue, but may withhold information that is necessary for an effort to cause you to fail.

Denial

Often the damage from emotional manipulation is inflicted after the fact. When you confront someone with evidence of their dishonesty and abuse, their refusal to admit wrongdoing can cause even greater psychological harm.

Rationalization

The increase in popular news media has led to the growth of public relations and marketing firms who produce "spin" to deflect criticism in both political and corporate environments. Rationalization is a form of spin, in which a manipulator explains away his or her abuse.

Minimization

Like rationalization, minimization is a form of denial in which the predator understates the seriousness of his or her offense.

Selective Attention and/or Inattention

Manipulators will pick and choose which parts of an argument or debate should be considered so that only their views are represented.

Diversion

Manipulators often resist giving straight answers to questions, particularly when they are confronted by their victims. Instead, they will divert the conversation to some other topic or change the subject altogether.

Evasion

More serious than a diversion, a manipulative person confronted with his or her own guilt will often completely evade responsibility by using long rambling responses filled with so-called "weasel words," like "most people would say," "according to my sources," or other phrases that falsely legitimize their excuses.

Covert Intimidation

Many manipulative people will make implied threats to discourage further inquiries or resolution.

Guilt-tripping

A true form of emotional manipulation, a manipulator will exploit the integrity and conscientiousness of the victim by accusing them of being too selfish, too irresponsible, or not caring enough.

Shaming

Although shaming can be used to bring about social change when large corporations or governments advance abusive or discriminatory policies, manipulators may attempt to intimidate their victims by using sharp criticism, sarcastic comments, or insults to make them feel bad.

Blaming the Victim

This tactic has become increasingly common. When a victim accuses a predator of abuse, the predator will attempt to turn it around by creating a scenario in which the victim alone is responsible for the harm that came to him.

Playing the Victim

Using the opposite tactic of blaming the victim, the predator will lure a conscientious person into a trap by pretending to have been grievously wounded and cultivating feelings of sympathy. The real plan, however, is to take advantage of the caring nature of the conscientious person by toying with their emotions.

Playing the Servant

This tactic is common in environments marked by a strict, well-established chain of command, like the military. Predators become skilled at manipulating this system by creating a persona of suffering and nobility, in which their bad actions are justified as a duty, obedience, and honor.

Seduction

This technique does not always have to involve sexual conquest or intimacy. Emotional predators may use flattery and charm to convince people to do their bidding, and they often look for people with low self-esteem.

Projection

This term is used in psychotherapy. Predators that use this technique will look for victims to use as scapegoats. When the manipulator does something wrong and is confronted, he or she will "project" his or her guilt onto the victim to make the victim look like the responsible party.

Feigning Innocence

This technique can be used as part of a strategy of denial. Under questioning, the manipulator will "play innocent" by pretending that any violation was unintentional, or that they were not the party who committed the violation.

Feigning Confusion

This technique can also be used as part of a strategy of denial. Under questioning, the manipulator will "play dumb" or pretend to be confused about the central point of the conflict or dispute. By creating confusion, the manipulator hopes to damage the confidence of his or her victim.

Peer Pressure

By using claims, whether true or not, that the victim's friends, associates, or "everyone else" is doing something, the manipulator will put pressure on his victim to change his or her behavior or attitude.

Signs That You're Being Manipulated

We are all potentially susceptible to emotional manipulation by people who show characteristic signs of dark psychology.

A very easy example can be Victimization: it can occur in our everyday relationships with co-workers, bosses and supervisors, family members, and significant others.

Emotional manipulation can also occur in professional relationships with people we may regard as normally trustworthy—such as sales representatives, government officials, and other representatives of institutions such as medical facilities, banks, businesses, schools, and law firms.

Emotional predators share one common trait: They look for people who are conscientious, dependable, loyal, honest, and reliable. People with these character traits are the easiest to manipulate because all the tricks in the manipulator's toolbox are designed specifically to take advantage of these emotional and psychological characteristics. More importantly, emotional predators lack empathy or morality. They do not regard their abuses as shocking or unacceptable; instead, they regard the overabundance of conscientious people as "job security" and a golden opportunity.

Emotional predators can be found in all walks of life. Throughout their lives, they have learned how to adapt, blend in, and even achieve high levels of professional and financial success in the "straight world."

Remember that having a valid and legitimate expectation that people will be honest in their dealings with you means that you are a conscientious person. Although you occupy the superior position, emotional predators are highly skilled at exploiting this expectation and avoiding detection and/or punishment.

As we have seen, emotionally manipulative people use a wide variety of techniques and methods to gain power in relationships. What's more, the people you are closest to and most familiar with—people whom you should be able to trust the most—are in the best position to use emotional manipulation to exploit and take advantage of your trust. In fact, establishing trust and familiarity is one of the most important aspects of a successful effort to exploit someone's emotional vulnerability, and then manipulate them either for personal gain or simply out of pure malice.

Of course, simply because this type of abuse has become common does not mean that you should automatically and necessarily regard all of your friends and trusted associates as predators and manipulators. Nor should you give in to the temptation to regard being conscientious, law-abiding, and honest as a problem. However, victims of emotional manipulation are often unaware that they are being exploited and abused, so it is important to learn how to recognize the signs of manipulation.

Specific Examples of Emotional Manipulation

- Insisting on meeting at certain locations: Manipulators may try to get the upper hand by insisting on a so-called "home-court advantage," thereby forcing you to function in a less familiar and less comfortable environment that diminishes your personal negotiating power. Examples:
  - If you have a dispute with a professional acquaintance or colleague, they may insist on always meeting in their office or at a café or restaurant that is more difficult for you to travel to.
- Premature intimacy or closeness: The manipulator will immediately shower you with affection and reveal all sorts of intimate secrets. Examples:
  - In a personal relationship, the manipulator may introduce themselves using phrases like, "No one has ever made me feel like this before. I know we were made for each other."
- Managing conversations by always requiring you to speak first: In professional relationships, this is commonly used as a sales and negotiation technique to mine you for your information to make a more lucrative sale. Examples:
  - A salesperson may say something like, "Rather than bore you with details about our products or services, why don't you tell me about yourself and how you think we can help you?"

- Distorting or twisting facts: Whether in personal or professional relationships, manipulators will use conversational techniques to distort facts to make you doubt yourself and back down. Example:
  - A manipulator may use a phrase like, "I understand how you feel. I'd be angry, too. But the truth is, I never made that comment. I don't think your memory of that conversation is accurate. I know what you really meant to say was that…"
- Intellectual bullying: An emotional manipulator may use an unnecessarily large volume of statistics, jargon, or other types of factual evidence to impose a sense of expertise.
- Bureaucratic bullying: This technique is similar to intellectual bullying. Unfortunately, this technique may indicate that someone is abusing their position of authority by insisting on placing as many obstacles, red tape, or other impediments in the way of what should be a straightforward resolution. Example:
  - Such a person may make a statement such as, "I understand your concerns, but I would encourage you not to pursue this any further. You have a legitimate complaint, but the expenses and time required will probably cost more than you will get in return.
- Passive aggression: There are many examples of passive-aggressive behavior in conversation in both personal and professional relationships to force you to back down to the predatory efforts of a manipulator. Example:

- A manipulator may try to make you feel bad for voicing your concerns by saying something along the lines of, "I understand that you are voicing an important objection, but have ever stopped to consider what will happen to the rest of the team if you eventually get your way?"
- Insults and put-downs: Manipulators are good at following up rude or mean-spirited comments with sarcasm or some other attempt at humor to make it seem like they were joking. Example:
- "I know you really worked hard on that presentation. It's too bad you wasted your time, though. But, hey, no worries. I'm sure it will be great preparation when you interview for your position."

Chapter 5: Victims

Just as manipulators frequently share all sorts of similar traits and behaviors, they also share similar taste in victims. Manipulators, like all predators, look for the easiest targets that pose the best chance of success. Just as the pack of wolves will pick off the weakest members of a herd, the manipulator will look for people who they deem are emotionally easy targets, using a sort of natural sense for whom to go after. Because they go for these specific traits, they are usually incredibly efficient in what they do. Manipulators have essentially mastered the art of picking up the perfect target. Take a look at some of the most commonly targeted traits, as well as the signs someone around you may be being abused or manipulated.

Traits of a Victim

While some manipulators may go out of their way to target other types of people, the vast majority will go for ease of a target overlooking for a challenge. When they are going to manipulate others, they want to make sure they can get away with it, as well as to get away with any of the behaviors they wish to expose the other person too. Some manipulators never move beyond emotional exploitation, while others will go out of their way to work their ways up to physical or sexual abuse. Ultimately, these are some of the easily exploitable traits that manipulators everywhere look for:

Empathetic

The perfect manipulation victim is empathetic. When they are empathetic, they are far easier to manipulate. Think back to the reason's manipulators tend to manipulate—one is to get what they want. An empath is going to be quick to tune into whatever it is that the other person needs, and is much more likely to want to give whatever it is, whether it is attention, affection, or companionship. This makes the empath an ideal target.

Further, empaths, especially if they meet some of the other criteria on this list, are frequently quite forgiving. They will be quick to write off some bad behavior as a fluke or an unfortunate consequence of the circumstances, and they will be more likely to believe that the manipulator will not continue the behaviors. They are also more likely to fall for guilt trips, making manipulating them somewhat easier than others. What the empath offers most of all is the patience necessary to put up with the manipulator's antics.

Caregiver

People with caregiver personalities thrive upon taking care of others. They love to make sure those around them have their needs met. They naturally care about what others need and are often also quite empathetic. Because they feel fulfilled taking care of the needs of others, manipulators can typically twist things around to get whatever they want. The manipulator is quite skilled at convincing the caregiver that he needs something he does not, and the caregiver, wanting to make sure the manipulator is cared for, will do so.

Caregivers, in particular, tend to be quite patient—they are willing to put up with far more than necessary simply because they feel they can handle it. They are likely to forego ending a relationship they see as abusive or manipulative if they believe that the cause of that abuse or manipulation is old wounds within the manipulator that are causing the behaviors in the first place. Instead, the caregiver will put up with the manipulation while diligently attempting to fix the manipulator's problems.

Codependent

Codependency and caregiver personalities are incredibly similar—both the codependent and the caregiver will pour themselves into their relationship, hoping to fix the manipulator, but the codependent will wholly identify with the relationship. The codependent is more likely to put up with far worse manipulation and abuse simply because she feels she cannot move on from the manipulator. While she may recognize what is happening, she feels so intricately intertwined with the manipulator and that relationship that she feels there is no life without the manipulator. Her very identity will be wrapped up in caring for the manipulator, catering to his every whim, even to her detriment. Even though it will hurt her, she continues to do so anyway to a fault. Her codependent nature becomes a point of contention for her as the relationship that she feels is all that she is also hurting her. She may not like the way she is being treated, but she will want to continue to pour herself into the relationship.

Grew Up in Dysfunction

Those who grew up in the throes of dysfunction oftentimes have skewed ideas of what normal is. They see the way they grew up as normal and will oftentimes revert back to what is familiar to them, even if familiar is harmful. For these people, they may see no red flags with the manipulator's behaviors, particularly if manipulation was one of the key features of their own dysfunctional upbringing.

Since they grew up around unhealthy relationships, their own tolerance for abuse is usually quite extreme. They may be annoyed, but see it as unworthy of ending a relationship or friendship. Even things like physical abuse may not be deal-breakers for those who grew up around it and had such abuse normalized for them. This makes them particularly easy targets because they will be so tolerant and already desensitized to too much of the abuse and manipulation that the manipulator will be utilizing.

Low Self-Esteem

Perhaps one of the most attractive of traits to a manipulator when looking for a victim is low self-esteem. You will learn that breaking someone's self-esteem is oftentimes a core theme in much of the manipulation you will be learning about. Manipulators need people with low self-esteem because they will not fight back or make things difficult—instead, they will put up with the abuse and accept whatever is being said simply because they do not have the self-esteem to trust themselves.

Because the first active step in much of the manipulation is usually breaking down self-esteem, manipulators love shortcuts. Just as how a wolf will go for the weakest in a herd, the manipulator will go for the easiest target, and frequently, those are the ones whose self-esteem is already so weak and shattered that they can do whatever they want with impunity.

Ultimately, the more of these traits that an individual has, the more attractive they are to the manipulator. With that in mind, if you feel like you see any of these signs in yourself, these are likely to be your weaknesses. If you know you have low self-esteem, for example, you should be aware of how that can work against you if you are not careful.

Signs of Abuse or Manipulation
Oftentimes, those who have been manipulated show very similar behavioral signs. After being victimized for so long, they pick up similar behavioral patterns in an attempt at self-preservation. Take a look at some of the most commonly exhibited signs and symptoms of manipulation.

Self-Sacrificing or Martyrdom
Those who have been manipulated enough oftentimes develop an attitude that they do not deserve to be taken care of. They see

themselves as expendable, not worth the effort it would take to do things for themselves. Rather than focusing on bettering themselves, they focus on making sure the manipulator is cared for, just as the manipulator intended. They will oftentimes give up whatever they are asked to do, or volunteer to be the one missing out simply because they have been conditioned to do so.

Self-Sabotage

Oftentimes, the victim becomes so accustomed to not getting what he or she wants that they will begin to believe they are not deserving of having needs met. They are so used to being seen as expendable and with their needs as unimportant that they will begin to act as such as well. If they get something nice, they will believe that they do not deserve it, which can convince them that they should do something to sabotage what they have. For example, if someone has just gotten a new job that pays well, he may decide that he does not deserve that job, and because he does not deserve that job, he would possibly perform poorly unconsciously, believing that he is not good enough anyway, so he has no point to bother trying.

Fiercely Protective of Abuser

People who are regularly exposed to abuse or manipulation frequently become fiercely defensive and protective of anyone they feel threatens them. Because the manipulator frequently convinces the victim that the victim is exceedingly lucky to have someone like the manipulator around, and intentionally manipulates the feelings of the other person in an attempt to trick the other person into falling in love, the victim often feels conflicting emotions when the manipulator is talked poorly about. Oftentimes, the victim will vehemently defend the manipulator to anyone who says something they disagree with, feeling the need to protect the manipulator.

Mental Health Issues

Through constant stress from the manipulator, it is not uncommon by any means for people to develop mental health issues. After extended periods of being manipulated, belittled, and demeaned for the manipulator to gain a sense of control over the individual being manipulated, the victim is more prone to depressive and anxiety symptoms.

Being Distrustful

After time spent being demeaned and manipulated, people tend to grow to be quite distrustful. Especially once they have come to discover the truth and they understand that someone they had trusted actually was using them in some of the worst ways imaginable, they lose the capacity to trust easily and readily.

Fearful Behavior

Because people who are manipulated often find themselves getting to a point where they fear the reaction of the manipulator if they do not concede to whatever the manipulator wants, the victims tend to grow fearful in general. They are so used to someone taking advantage of the situation and making them feel bad about themselves when they are not living up to expectations that they often come to expect the worst from others as well. They grow timid and concerned with assuming that people around them have the worst intentions, and that leads to a fearful demeanor, especially when the victim perceives that he or she has failed in some way.

Paranoia

Typically, in a combination of becoming fearful and distrustful, those who are manipulated sometimes develop a paranoid view of the world. They worry that they are being taken advantage of, even when they are not, and they become inherently suspicious of those who do try to help, assuming there is some sort of ulterior motive at play when someone does offer help. For example, if a manipulation victim is asked if she wants help with studying for an upcoming exam, she may wonder what the other person wants in return, even if the other person is simply doing it out of kindness or a genuine interest in getting to know her better with no strings attached.

Chapter 6: Stop the Manipulators

Many manipulators will do their best to make sure that the victim doesn't realize what's happening, but there are ways to use this to your advantage.

By creating stakes, the manipulator has control over you because they know that either way they win. During those stakes, it's important to recognize that they don't expect you to not play their game.

A manipulator knows how to use dark psychology to make the victim do what they ask. If they are constantly picking on you or taking note of every mistake you've ever made, the manipulator is planning to use this against you. Their reactions to the things that disappoint them are important too.

Pay attention to how they respond to you in the beginning because this will change as time passes. The manipulator will take note of how you react to things not going your way. If you are prone to fits of rage yourself when frustrated, the manipulator will know how to use that against you. If you get depressed or are deeply saddened by failure, the manipulator will use that against you. Dark psychology focuses on human reaction to situations and using that to influence a situation.

A manipulator will focus on every reaction, every moment of joy, sadness, or anger, and twist it to suit their needs. For example,

Liam and Cierra are brother and sister. Liam wants Cierra to stay home from summer camp this year because he doesn't want her to ruin his summer. Liam knows that Cierra doesn't like Sarah D. from her grade and would do anything to avoid her. Liam tells Cierra that this year Sarah is going to be at the summer camp and she's going to be bunking in her cabin. Cierra not wanting to spend a whole summer sleeping in the same room as Sarah drops out of the summer camp, and now Liam gets to go alone as he wanted. Something as simple as knowing that his sister didn't like another student was all he needed to manipulate her into doing what he wanted.

It's easy to manipulate someone into doing what you ask when you know what grinds their gears. Using dark psychology could make it easier for a manipulator to take advantage, and the victim wouldn't know how they allowed them to use these weaknesses.

Narcissistically, they would believe they are smarter than their victim and pay close attention to how they react to even the manipulator themselves. Manipulators love over-sharers or people who don't care who knows about their lives. These people are easier to manipulate because they lay everything about them on the table.

For example, Tyra is always talking about her bad marriage to John, John's friend that wants to have sex with Tyra knows how bad his marriage to his wife is and knows how John acts. Hence, he portrays the exact opposite of that and manipulates Tyra into sleeping with him by complaining about his friendship with John.

A manipulator will always make things go their way by using keywords that may trigger a response out of the victim. They may berate them constantly for something small or make them feel guilty for having any reaction to what's happening around them at all. A manipulator's main tool to anything is pulling the wool over the victim's eyes. Dark persuasion is making the victim feel like they have no control over the situation or giving all the "power" to the victim. Prolonging events or constant empty promises may occur.

The manipulator will always show that they are in complete control, but it's up to the victim to say they aren't falling for it. They will find ways to make it feel like the victim has the power of choice, but the manipulator has carefully thought out every step from the moment they picked their victim.

Dark persuasion considers age, creed, upbringing, religion, and/or sexuality. The manipulator will take all these factors and create a trap for their victim. The victim would be completely unaware of what's happening, but they will feel like the events are correlated with their behavior or with what's happening as the situation transpires.

They won't be able to see how the manipulator has taken control of what's happening and leads them to do what they ask of them without much question. The manipulator is skilled at masking their true intentions of what they are doing, and the victim won't see they are being manipulated.

For example, Marie wants Donny to pay for her to go to Miami. She knows that Donny never got to travel because of his parents not being able to afford it, so she makes him feel bad that she can't afford it. Donny doesn't realize that she is doing this just to get her way and agrees to pay for the trip. Marie has known Donny for a few months and knew that from conversations they had together that something like that would work.

When unmasking the true intentions of another person, you must consider the person that you are dealing with. Sometimes you feel like they are manipulating the situation and when you feel that way, it's good to step up. However, if you can't identify the manipulation, one way is to focus on the person's choice of words.

If they are constantly repeating something or constantly return to one specific phrase in a spiral during a conflict, they are concentrating the focus on what they want. Look out for how they react to simple requests, something simple can become a chore for someone that is trying to manipulate a situation and they will use these repeated words or actions to get a rise of out the victim.

For example, Duncan doesn't want to do the dishes, so he complains to his sister about how he must do dishes all the time at work and that he gets cuts on his hands whenever he does them from the silverware and cutlery. Every time he doesn't want to do dishes, this is what Duncan will say and his sister will do it because she doesn't want her brother to suffer.

However, once she noticed that he only does this when he must do them, she eventually told him that she is no longer doing it. Once you recognize that you are being manipulated, it's easier to prevent it from continuing.

Manipulators may also get angry over very little things, to make themselves look and feel bigger. They will start fights over someone not listening to them or they will start a fight over the way a person looks at them.

A manipulator will shout, especially when they know they are in the wrong and don't want to admit it. As mentioned, if they feel cornered or don't know how to make themselves look like the victim, shouting is the next method. If someone for no reason just explodes, the fear they incite can make someone do what they want.

For example, Lorne wants Greg to stop asking him about why he came home late from work. Greg accuses him of cheating, Lorne tosses his coat down onto the floor and starts shouting at Greg for yelling at him when he's tired and has been working. Greg backs down because he is afraid of what would happen if he continued to yell at Lorne. And Lorne knew that Greg would if he yelled at him because Greg came from an abusive household. By knowing that piece and information and knowing his husband's reactions, Lorne can manipulate Greg and get what he wants.

It's these small interactions that manipulators need most, so pay close attention to how many questions they ask about your life. And pay attention to how much they share with you after they get the answers they want.

A manipulator would be hyper curious about your life or your friends or family. The victim would voluntarily share this with a boyfriend/girlfriend/partner, maybe even a close friend. If the manipulator seems to provide nothing to contribute to the stream of information they get, be careful with what is shared.

For example, Tammy knows everything about Veronika's life, but Veronika knows nothing about hers. Tammy would always ask her best friend to talk about her life, but Veronika would provide little to nothing in retort. It's important to pay close attention to that information as well.

It could be basic, easily relatable topics to avoid talking about their real life and intentions. Or they could even set up for manipulation in the future by planting false stories about their lives into the conversation.

Manipulators will make sure that the victim is dependent purely on them, constantly creating a situation where they would be the higher authority and not be able to lose the rank they have over the victim. Taking them out of their comfort zone would be the most important part.

They would never let them go to a place where the victim could be superior.

For example, Frank doesn't want to go with Amy to her favorite diner. Frank prefers his diner because he's the important one and they care more about him than they would his date. He also wants Amy to think he's better than what she believes he is. Frank talks up the diner and convinces Amy to go with him to the diner. Being in that diner, Amy hears stories about Frank's childhood and learns only about the parts of his life that Frank wants her to know. A manipulator will censor the content that is available to you and make it impossible for you to look past the manipulation.

Censoring what you know can also come in the form of overusing information. A manipulator will spend more time correcting you. They will question your intelligence and won't believe you if you claim to know any information. To the manipulator, the victim is always wrong and doesn't know anything.

They will do whatever they can to make sure the only information the victim ever receives comes from them. Pay attention to how much they correct the small things you do; watch the number of times this occurs and watch how they do it.

A manipulator might prevent them from going online or checking their phones or would get mad at them for trying to source check any information they come across during the relationship.

For example, Tom is with Jane. Tom doesn't want Jane to know anything about his past and gets angry with her every time she tries to look up anything. Tom deleted all photos on his social media accounts that had any inkling of him having any former partners as well as his old drug use. Tom doesn't want Jane to see anything before she started seeing him, and when she asks about his past, Tom tells Jane he was a good student and didn't get into any trouble.

Chapter 7: Dark Criminals among Us

Before a person orchestrates something malicious, they may have thought about everything for a prolonged period, for instance, in the case of a mass shooting. The perpetrator's main motive may be unknown; however, it is evident upon investigation that such people have usually engaged in negative behaviors that are harmful to others close to them.

Some researchers, such as James Alan Fox and Monica J. DeLateur in their paper Mass Shootings in America: Moving beyond Newtown (2013), have looked into the matter, and the difficulty of identifying a potential mass shooter in advance, especially at a tender age. Nevertheless, it is evident that there are some thinking patterns and behaviors that usually manifest with time, and educators also encounter them since they spend a considerable amount of time with pupils. The parents are also familiar with each of these patterns. The main hope is that the children who exhibit each of these traits can outgrow them, eventually. Some children do; however, some do not outgrow these traits, and they can harm the people around them. When the patterns intensify, it is important to seek help, and we cannot wait for a seriously malicious action to occur.

When a person engages in crime at a tender age, it is a sign that there is some trouble ahead; not necessarily a mass shooting;

however, the behaviors of such people may result in other people being financially, emotionally, and physically hurt.

People with Dark Triad traits may also engage in lying while also blaming other people for their misfortunes. The parents and teachers may not have the ability to control some of the choices that the children make; nevertheless, they may have noticed some warning signs.

Although Dark Triad traits manifest over time, children who simply exhibit some of these traits cannot be labeled as "criminals," since they have not done anything wrong. Since the children are still young, they may still be learning about the world, and they can develop more understanding and empathy as they grow. They can turn out as good, well-rounded people, so it is important to support and work with them, without labeling children negatively.

Children are delicate beings, and they should be molded accordingly. When a child is born, people strive to look into whether the child may have learning problems, physical disabilities, and emotional problems. We should also strive to ensure that we have identified other problems that the children may be suffering from so that they cannot injure their peers or because any harm to themselves, since they do not have any sense of responsibility at a young age, this comes with learning and maturity.

The mental health system should be improved. There should be some strict background checks, and gun laws should also be revised. We should also focus more on identifying some of the "errors" present in the thinking process. We all possess enough knowledge about how we can help children who show potentially harmful traits. The children can be mentored accordingly, and they can hopefully develop more positive traits in the future. Always embark on such a mission with sensitivity and compassion.

Criminal Mind vs. Cybercriminal Mind

The study is related to criminal anthropology, and it delves deep into what drives someone into becoming a criminal. Additionally, the study also looks into a person's reactions after committing a crime.

Criminal psychologists are frequently called up to the stand in court so that they may serve as witnesses since they have an in-depth understanding of the criminal mind. There are different types of psychiatry, and they also deal with some aspects of criminal behavior. It is, however, somewhat difficult to define the criminal mind.

The Role of Psychology in the Legal System

Psychologists and psychiatrists are normally professionals who are licensed, and they are tasked with assessing the physical and mental state of a person. There are also profilers, and they are tasked with looking for patterns in a person's behavior as they try to identify the person who took part in a certain crime. Some group efforts also focus more on attempting to answer different "common" psychological questions. If a sexual offender is about to commit a re-offending act after being put back into society, how can such an issue be handled? Other issues that arise include; is the sexual offender fit enough to take the stand in court? Was the offender sane when they were committing the offense?

A criminal psychologist may be required to undertake investigative tasks such as examining photographs that were taken at a crime scene. They can also be tasked with interviewing the victim and the suspect. At times, a criminal psychologist comes up with a hypothesis to assess what the offender might do after being released after they have completed their sentence.

The question about a person's competency to stand trial depends on the offender's state of mind as they engaged in the criminal act, and when they are about to take the stand in court. The criminal psychologist will have to assess the ability of the offender to understand the charges that have been placed against them and the possible outcomes that may arise after they are convicted. The offender should also have the ability to offer some assistance to their attorneys as they defend them in court.

The question of criminal responsibility is aimed at assessing the criminal's state of mind as they committed the crime. The main focus is on whether they understand the difference between what is right and wrong and anything that is against the law. The insanity defense is not commonly used, since it cannot be proved easily. If a person succeeds with the insanity defense, they will be sent to a secure hospital facility for a long period as compared to the period that they would have served in prison.

The Roles of a Criminal Psychologist

The roles of a legal psychologist are as follows:

Clinical

In such an instance, the psychologist is supposed to assess an individual so that they can issue a clinical judgment. The psychologist can make use of different assessment tools, psychometric tools, or they can take part in a normal interview with the offender. After that, they are supposed to make an informed decision depending on the outcome of the interview. The assessment comes in handy since it can help the police and other organizations to determine how the offender, in this case, will be processed. For instance, the clinical psychologist can find out whether the offender is sane so that they can stand trial. They can also determine whether the offender has a mental illness, which relates to whether they are capable of understanding the court proceedings.

Experimental

In this instance, the psychologist is tasked with carrying out some research about the case. They can perform some experiments so that they can illustrate a certain point while also providing further information that will be presented as evidence in court. They may carry out eyewitness credibility and false memory assessments. For instance, they can try to assess whether an eyewitness can spot an object that is 100 meters away.

Advisory

A psychologist is supposed to advise the police about how they should proceed with the investigation. For instance, they can weigh into matters such as which is the best way to interview an eyewitness and the offender. They can also weigh into matters such as how an offender may act after committing a crime.

Actuarial

This is where the psychologist makes use of statistics so that they can inform a case. For instance, they can be tasked with providing the probability of an event taking place. The court may also consider the likelihood of a person engaging in certain acts such as defiling another person sexually after they have served their jail term or after they have been released if the evidence against them was not strong enough.

Profiling

Criminal profiling is also referred to as offender profiling. It is the process of linking the actions of an offender to the crime scene. The offender's characteristics will also ensure that the police can prioritize and narrow down all possibilities when considering all the possible suspects. Profiling is quite new concerning forensic psychology. The field of forensic psychology has grown in the past two decades. Initially, it was an art. Currently, it is a rigorous science. There are different sub-fields in forensic psychology, including investigative psychology. Criminal profiling currently entails carrying out some intensive research and also carrying out some rigorous methodological advances.

Criminals are usually classified based on factors such as sex, age, physical characteristics, geographic region, and education. When comparing some of the similar characteristics, you can easily understand a criminal's motivation when they decide to partake in criminal behavior.

Some national and international security organizations, including the FBI, usually refer to "criminal profiling" as "criminal investigative analysis." The analysts or profilers are normally trained. During the training process, they learn more about the behavioral aspects of different people and also learn more about the details of unsolved violent crime scenes, whereby there are some traces of psychopathy at the scene where the crime was committed.

The general appearance of the crime scene. It may be organized or disorganized.

The profiler can go ahead and interpret the behavior of the offender based on the crime scene. They can discuss everything further with their counterparts.

As a criminal psychologist, you may have to consider profiling from a racial perspective. Race plays a major role in the criminal justice system. In the past few years, the state and federal prisons have held more than 475,900 black inmates. The number of white inmates totaled 436,500. The difference is quite significant. Some of the black people are in prison because of negative stereotypes. Such stereotypes are ineffective, and some criminal psychologists can ascertain that the race of a person does not contribute to them being violent.

There are environmental, cultural, and traditional concepts that surround each race. Each of these concepts plays a key role in psychology. Some people may lack equal opportunities as a result of race or gender, for example, and that means that they have fewer chances to thrive.

Applied Criminal Psychology
For a criminal psychiatrist, the main question is, "Which offender will become a patient?" and "Which patient will become an offender?" Other questions that a psychiatrist should ask themselves are, "Which came first, the mental disorder or the crime?" Psychologists should take a look into the environmental factors and the genetics of a person while they carry out the profiling, to help determine whether the suspect committed the crime or not.

Some of the questions that criminal psychologists should ask themselves include:

- Is the mental disorder present at the moment? Did the person have a mental disorder when they were engaging in the criminal act?
- What is the level of responsibility of the person who committed the crime?
- Is treatment the best option when trying to reduce the risks of re-offending?
- Is there a possibility that the offender may engage in another crime, and what are the risk factors in this case?

The individual psychiatric evaluations normally come in handy since they help to measure an offender's personality traits through psychological testing. The results can also be presented in court.

The Dark Triad

The notion that dark psychology is prevalent and that it is part of our world can be a scary thought. The Dark Triad is a term in dark psychology that can be helpful when trying to pinpoint the beginning of criminal behavior.

Narcissism exhibits these traits: egotism, grandiosity, and lack of empathy.

Machiavellianism uses a form of manipulation to betray and exploit people. Those who practice this do not practice morality or ethics.

Psychopathy is a trick to those who put their trust in these types of people. They are often charming and friendly. Yet they are ruled by impulsivity, selfishness, lack of empathy, and remorselessness.

The fact that people can be used as pawns on a chessboard makes all of us want to understand dark psychology more and to figure out what it is, and how we can save ourselves from it.

There are many ailments that hypnosis can make better or even cure. And we are not just talking about mental ailments, but physical as well. Hypnosis can be used to help cure some of the side effects that are caused by chemo and radiation in cancer patients.

We all know that there has been a lot of skepticism for this alternative medicine due to the quacks that use it as a laughingstock. However, when used correctly, this type of medicine can do a lot better than harm because it wakes people's subconscious up to letting go of things that they are holding on to that might be causing a plethora of problems in their lives.

With this being said, all of these methods can be used for good; it is just based on their intentions and the overall outcome. Those who use manipulation tactics do not use them to help anyone. Manipulating is changing someone's thoughts, actions, and behaviors to fit someone else's (the manipulator's agenda). There is no way to sugarcoat some of these techniques. And that is why they fall under the dark psychology umbrella because they have been used by criminals to get what they want as well.

Because we all know that someone is going to try to make us a victim of one of these methods again, sometime in our lives, and I for one would want to be as ready as I could possibly be.

There are many examples of manipulation, mind control, and persuasion in history. Some of the most infamous examples are Charles Manson, Adolph Hitler, and Ted Bundy. When you look at Charles Manson, you can get a profile of someone who was able to use his words and "love" for his "family" to create a cult. He was able to take young adults and make them into murders. You need to remember that Charles Manson never actually killed anyone. He simply had the members of his "family" do this through manipulation, mind control, and persuasion.

Adolph Hitler was the same way. He started by getting people to like him through persuasion. People believed that he would be one of the greatest political leaders of all time. While he did go down in history, it is not because he was a great political leader.

Chapter 8: How the Mind Works When It Is Manipulated

When it comes to working with dark manipulation, there are going to be a lot of different methods and techniques that we can use to get what you want. Remember, we are talking about some forms of manipulation that are going to help us to get what we want but may end up harming the other person in the process. This means that they may not be seen as the best options to work with, and you may feel a bit uncomfortable with them if you have not worked in dark manipulation, or even with dark persuasion, in the past.

However, working with these techniques will help you to get the results that you want. They will ensure that the other person you are using as your target will be likely to do the actions or say the things that you would like them to, even though it may not be in their best interests to do so. With that said, let's take a look at some of the different dark manipulation tactics that you can use to get someone else to do what you want.

Using Isolation to Get What You Want

They like to spend some time talking with others, spending time out in public, having close friends, and family, and spending their time in more social situations. When we take this social aspect away from many individuals, it changes the way that they look at life.

Complete physical isolation can be the most powerful. This is when the subject is taken away from all contact with others, including email, social media, phone calls, and physical contact. This is something that has been seen in cults and with other groups. They will often take the person far away from others, and then the only human contact that the person can have is with the captors.

Now, this total physical isolation can be really hard to do, and it is usually only done in really intense situations. If you are just trying to use manipulation, you usually don't want to go through and completely isolate the target. But it is common for a manipulator will typically try to attempt their target mentally as much as possible.

There are several methods that the manipulator can use to get what they want with the help of manipulation. They could include some seminars that last a week in the country and isolate the person from what they would usually do. They could be a lot of criticisms of the person's family and close friends so that the target feels bad and stops seeing them. It could be jealousy that keeps the target at home and limits the amount of influence that anyone outside the manipulator has on the person.

Once the manipulator can control the information that goes to the target, they can share information, withhold information, and do anything that they would like to continue influencing the target as much as they would like. The target is going to become reliant on the manipulator, and this is how the manipulator can work and get what they want from the target. There are no outside influences to tell the target that something is wrong, or that they should watch out, and this ensnares the target even more.

Criticism

The next option to work with when it comes to manipulation is the idea of using criticism. This one is sometimes used with isolated or on its own and it works well because it makes the target feel like they are always doing something wrong, and that they are not able to meet the high standards of the manipulator. The criticism can always show up on a variety of topics and could include how they look, who they hang out with, the clothes they wear, their beliefs, and anything that the manipulator thinks will work for this.

When a manipulator decides to use this tactic, they are going to be really good at hiding it behind one of their compliments to the other person. Or they will say something nice and add this little jab at the end of it. This allows them to say all the mean things that they want, and then they can say that the target misheard or misunderstood them and that they hadn't really meant any harm by it. This puts the target in a bad spot because they know the manipulator is being mean to them, but they are the ones who look paranoid and bad in this situation.

The criticism that the manipulator is going to use is often going to be small. They don't want to start out using really big criticisms that are obvious because the target doesn't want to be criticized. If the manipulator starts out with something big, the target is going to fight back and walk away. But when it starts out small with some little comments along the way, it starts to plant a bit of self-doubt, something that the target is going to notice, but they often are not going to fight back against.

They are going to start out with something that may seem like a compliment or like that is going to sound like they are being helpful, but in reality, they are trying to be hurtful in the process. They may say something like, "I didn't know that you liked the color blue. I think you should go with something else." This one is going to have the hidden meaning inside of it that you don't look good in what you are wearing, and your clothes don't look that well.

Or maybe you bring in your favorite outfit to a meeting to make yourself feel better. You are excited and you feel really good about the way that you look and feel in the outfit. But then they are going to say something about how they liked you in some other outfit better. It isn't necessarily mean, but it is said in a manner and at a time that it ends up hurting your feelings in the process.

As time goes on, the type of criticism that is going to be used against the target is going to get worse. And the criticism is going to become quite a bit more obvious as well to add in a bit more self-doubt here. This is going to make it so that the target starts to rely on the manipulator a bit more. This is because the target is going to feel like they have so many flaws that are hard to ignore, and that the only person who can like them and maybe even love them, through these flaws will be the manipulator. The fact that the manipulator is still around is a good sign that they care, and this causes the target to be more willing to do what the manipulator asks.

The manipulator is going to find that they can use this criticism more of us against them kind of idea if it works better as well. They could even choose to move their criticism to be against the outside world so that they can claim they are more superior.

When this happens, the manipulator is going to claim to their target that they are super lucky that the manipulator is even associating with them. The manipulator will ensure that they are important so that the target is more likely to stick around and do what they want. This alone is meant to be enough if it is done in the right manner so that the target feels lucky just because the manipulator is going to spend time with them.

Alienating the Target to Get What They Want

No one wants to be alienated. They want to feel like they are a part of the group. They want to feel accepted, as they belong, and more. This is never more apparent than when we see a newcomer. When someone is new to town, or to school, to work, or somewhere else, you will notice that they are trying to figure out how to join the group and get them to accept them. They are worried that they are going to be alienated and to avoid this, they will do everything in their powers to get others to like them and go along with them, and this is where the manipulator can come in and get what they want.

Newcomers who start to join a new manipulative group are usually going to receive a very warm welcome.

There are several reasons for this one. First, this gets the target to feel welcome and more indebted to the group and the manipulator. They are thankful that they have these deep connections, and it is usually easier to get a friend to go along with something that a stranger, so it works to the benefit of the manipulator as well. Add in that the target is scared to be alienated, then they are going to do what they can to keep the relationships going strong.

If any doubts end up arising, these relationships are going to become a powerful tool to ensure they stay with the group. Even if they aren't completely convinced, the target will start to remember their outside world, the world that they had before joining this group, and it is going to seem cold and lonely. They will instead choose to stay with the group, even if there is some manipulation going on.

Simply because we do not want to be taken away from the crowd and we don't want others to have anything to do with us, we are going to do what the manipulator wants us to. The fact that humans are very social creatures and like to be included in some kind of group all the time, it is likely that we are going to give in to these urges to do what the manipulator wants, even if we don't feel like it is the best thing for us.

Using Social Proof as a Form of Peer Pressure

We like it when we are able to be a part of the group. Sometimes we center this on wanting to fit in, and we will follow the rules and do what we can to make sure that we are liked and part of the group. And even when we are more introverted and don't want to be in the group all the time, we still want to find a group of people we can be around and fit in. The thing is that the manipulator can come in here and use the idea of wanting to fit in to help them work against you and get you to do things that you don't want to.

Conclusion

Now that you have finished this book, you have become familiar with the common scenarios and tactics used by malicious users of dark psychology, and you have understood the difference between the personality types of the dark triad. You can use this information, not only as a defense against users of dark psychology but also as a way to probe and measure whether the people you interact with daily are sincere or simply trying to deceive those around them.

People are not always what they appear to be, and this message must be ingrained in the minds of people from all walks of life. Nothing is "too much" when it comes to dark psychology, and now, you are familiar with the thought that it's used every day by people who do not necessarily have bad intentions and who are not actively trying to deceive. Sometimes, emotional reactions and behaviors can influence our behavior in ways we don't understand unless we have researched and practiced awareness of ourselves and our actions daily. Do those whom you love and trust a favor by reaching out and sharing with them the knowledge you have gained from this book.

www.ingramcontent.com/pod-product-compliance
Lightning Source LLC
Chambersburg PA
CBHW062146100526
44589CB00014B/1701